BLACK RIVER

BY THE SAME AUTHOR

The Well: New and Selected Poems,
 2000 (Wolsak and Wynn)
Void and Voice: Essays on Literary and Historical Currents,
 1998 (Mosaic)
Clusters, 1997 (Mosaic)
Open to Currents, 1992 (Wolsak and Wynn)
Jackson's Point, 1989 (Oberon)
The Book of Salt, 1987 (Oberon)
Black Flamingo, 1985 (Mosaic)
Words for Elephant Man, 1983 (Mosaic)
The Cost of Living, 1981 (Mosaic)
Snake Music, 1979 (Mosaic)

KENNETH SHERMAN

BLACK RIVER

The Porcupine's Quill

Library and Archives Canada Cataloguing in Publication

Sherman, Kenneth, 1950–
    Black River / Kenneth Sherman.

A poem.
ISBN-13: 978-0-88984-289-2

    I. Title.

PS8587.H3863B53 2007   C811'.54   C2007-900140-8

Copyright © Kenneth Sherman, 2007.
1   2   3   4   •   09   08   07

Published by The Porcupine's Quill, 68 Main St, Erin, Ontario N0B 1T0. http://www.sentex.net/˜pql

Readied for the press by Eric Ormsby.
Copy edited by Doris Cowan.

All rights reserved. No reproduction without prior written permission of the publisher except brief passages in reviews. Requests for photocopying or other reprographic copying must be directed to Access Copyright.

Represented in Canada by the Literary Press Group.
Trade orders are available from University of Toronto Press.

We acknowledge the support of the Ontario Arts Council and the Canada Council for the Arts for our publishing program. The financial support of the Government of Canada through the Book Publishing Industry Development Program is also gratefully acknowledged. Thanks, also, to the Government of Ontario through the Ontario Media Development Corporation's OMDC Book Fund.

for Gordon Barrie

'He said to him: All powers of God are disposed in layers
and they are like a tree: just as the tree produces its fruit through water,
so God through water increases the power of the tree.
    And what is God's water?
It is *hokhmah* (wisdom) and the fruit of the tree is the soul
of the righteous who fly from the source to the great river ...'
                                                                     — The Bahir

'Everything flows; nothing remains'
                        — Herakleitos (fragment 20)

(Note: The Black River flows from the Oak Ridges Moraine,
through the town of Sutton, into Lake Simcoe.)

1

No mask.
Only me
and this throbbing artery.

2

By night, the Huron called it Star-Gatherer.
By day, Reflector-of-Many-Faces.

3

I lean over the gunwale
and catch my double,
auspicious, lamentable.
A Noh mask
presiding over the
nothing new, the all new.

4

Shall I paddle on like Radisson?
Shall I lie down in the belly of the boat,
protected by bulrushes,
trusting as Moses?
Best to exert the will of the wood-runner
while dreaming of a promised land
even if your fate is to land
at the dry, abridged docks of Sutton.

5

And you, Moses Cordovero,
you, Azriel of Gerona,
take me into the tree —
not the green mindless multitudes
beyond the bank, but the one with meaning,
sustained by spirit.

For there was damage done
on the shores of Simcoe
in that small habitation.

The wound unspoken.

6

All around you, the discontinuous.
But you continue, dark river, while the gods and goddesses
fall from the void like shredded texts —
the clouds, imageless.

7

In youth they massed into the recognizable.
and I flowed with the rush of you,
cut free from family,
my fishing rod resting at a 45-degree angle,
my bait preserved under the shadow of the thwart.
I was setting out for new territory.
Or so I supposed.
                  The angler
perpetually content with expectation,
fresh beginnings,
the electric quiver at the end of the line.

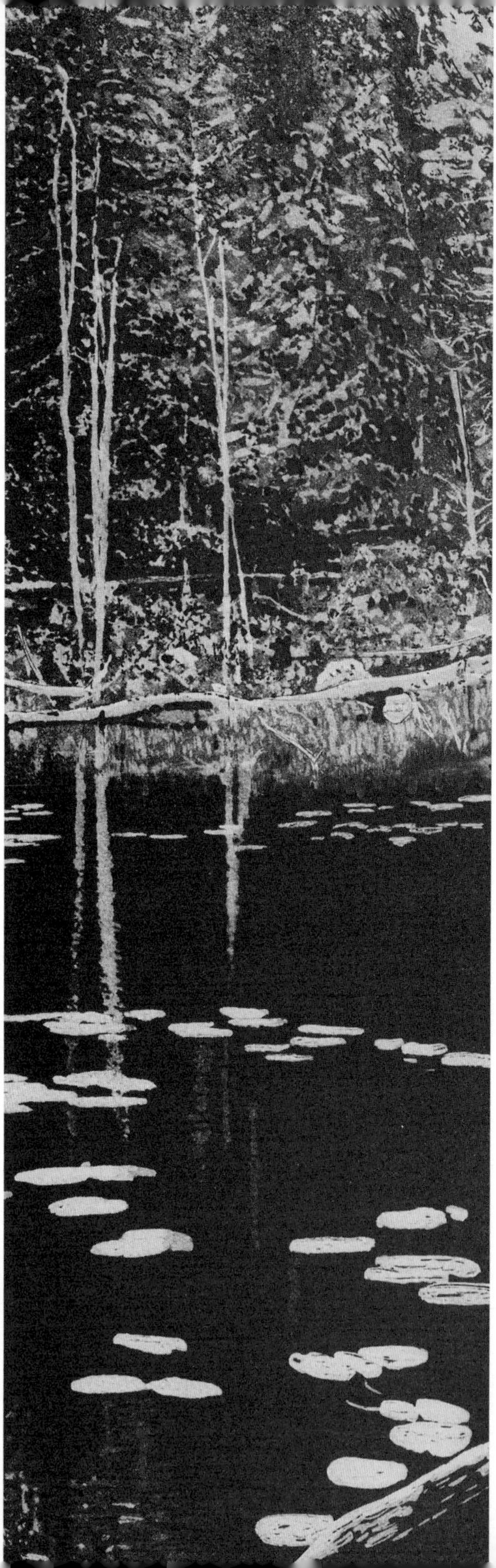

8

Bright dream mid-century. No antennae
littering the landscape. Only
a dim sense of post-war terror:
the park by the public pier,
immigrants with their coolers and caps —
a glimpse of their pale forearms,
the shock of their blue
numeral tattoos.

Thick accents
of the remnant.

9

And metres away Georgina's oldest church,
squatting on blanched limestone.
In its shaded cemetery,
Mazo de la Roche's lake view lot,
laughing Leacock in his family grave,
sunshine etched on his unpretentious stone.

10

I stood, a visitor
beneath St. George's brooding rafters,
the ethereal light pouring green and mauve
through stained glass
onto my foreign flesh

while down the road
our small synagogue in unassuming brick
protected by maples.

Gutturals and Eastern intuitions,
the desert God's undying voice —
in this landscape
subversive.
           Hidden.

11

Mon Coeur. The forests at Simcoe
cleared for development. Prosperity
and the end of identity.
The heavens drained
but better understood.

12

La Rivière Noire. The seraphs of industry
have raised their swords
pressing us into the new millennium
where nature is a microbe in an office vent.
Benny Big Canoe and his children
scrambling for menial jobs
in the village of my youth.

13

I read their ancestors' names in the registry.
Heroes of the War of 1812
rewarded with land,
now relegated to a reservation.
Reserve the nation. But for whom?

14

Stare out toward Georgina, Snake, and Thorah,
those distant, opalescent islands.
There, the native bands.
There, the great reduction.
Thirty thousand of the indigenous
near Simcoe's green shores,
powerless against the virus
dispensed by servants of Jesus.
The Big Canoes' halting syllables —
broken syntax
of the remnant.

15

1956. Our town's cigar-store wooden Indian,
his profile cracked, Semitic,
darkened with decades of weather,
enduring winter's long freeze-up.
In summer, he warded off ridicule with his solemn stare
fixed on the small park across the road
and on the towering ancient totem.
Sunday afternoons, our brass band
struggled with show tunes — *Oklahoma!* in Georgina,
played out beneath gigantic beaks
and the accusatory eyes of mythic birds.

16

And there I was
oblivious to history, oblivious to September 1793
when John Graves Simcoe and his Queen's Rangers
came upon *Quentaran* (beautiful water)
Ashuniong (place of the dog call).
and *Quah-so-quah-ming*.
The rippled soundings.

17

Simcoe's plan — to turn Upper Canada
into 'little England'. *Ko-te-quo-gong*
became London. *Shon-to-kay*,
the Humber. *Quay-te-kew*, the Don.
Mohawk chief Joseph Brant: 'General Simcoe
has done a great deal for our land.
He has changed the name of every place in it.'

Sarcasm
from the margins.

18

But take a deep breath:
It might have been worse.
Sim has a smooth sound. Watery.
And *Coe* is fish-like. Cold.

19

Shall I paddle on Radisson?
And let us not forget Groseilliers —
our boyhood's radishes and gooseberries.
Our textbook's buckskin-brown and beef-red illustrations:
natives torturing Jesuits,
devouring the heart of bravery,
but never a word about Micmacs —

no register
of the general slaughter.

20

O Dreamland. Fallen leaves. Tin
Mounties and maple sugar. Forgetfulness
and nightmare blood below the surface.

21

And myself, soon to be unmoored,
le bateau ivre,
adrift down the current of my unbecoming.
Dark water of words, syllabic silt,
moonless river within the river.
Redemption perhaps in your rush
over rock, your bullfrog gospel,
your late night liturgical hush.

22

O where does current come from?
From self-exile, self-banishment,
dark void drawing the darkening waters.

Not from seeded clouds.
Not from leached furrows.
Not from the diamond-cut heart
of glacier

but from the river below the river
God's own Gulag
the retractable Angel
of the Nothing pool
rushing
to greet something.

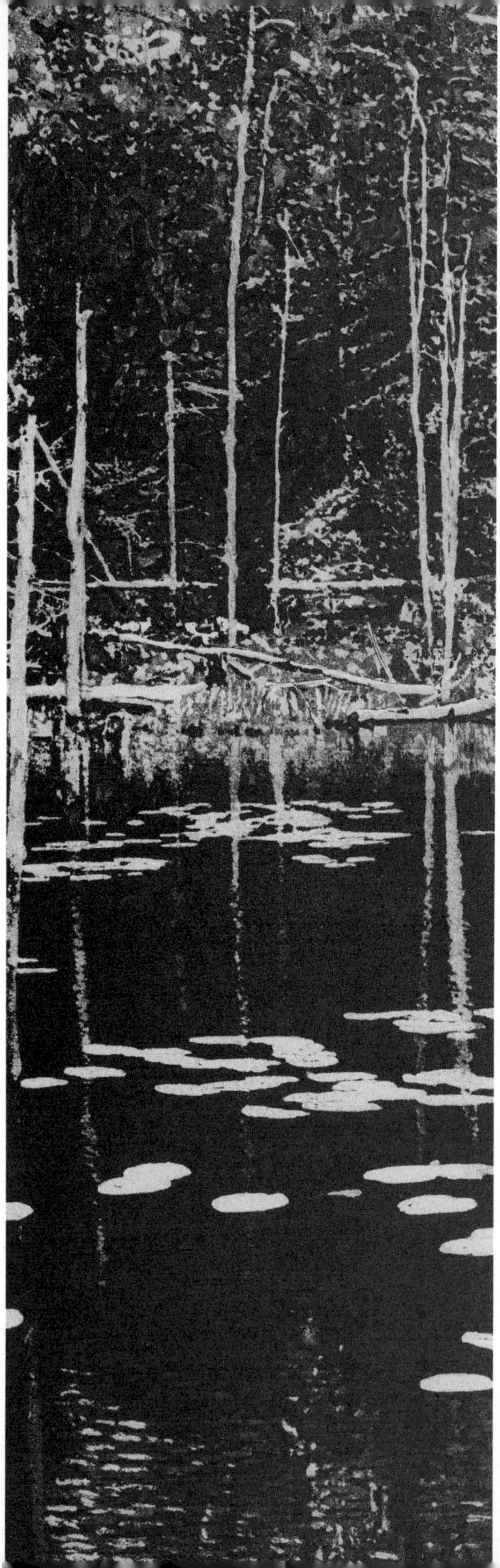

23

Near here, Grew developed its Fairmile B,
gorgeous instrument of war.
Magnificent WW II sub-hunter
built of mahogany, oak, teak,
carrying depth charges,
devices for sounding.
For listening.

Frog men in training
diving off the pier's blond planks.
You cannot hear them now
groaning in the surf of Juno Beach,
back-burdened with war gear.

You cannot listen in
to their death labour.

24

The deep and gloomy meadows.
Anderson's white truck,
the word ICE in letters of frosted blue.
He'd pull up the gravel path
and with monster tongs
wrestle the giant cubes.
His children accompanied him:
The girl, blonde, smelled like lemon suckers.
The boy resembled an illustration out of
my birthday copy of *Huckleberry Finn*.
Shy, they huddled by the doorway.
All three, gone through thin ice:
the startling crack and panic.
The white truck —
a four-wheeled mausoleum
settling on Simcoe's sodden floor.

25

What were they after?
Ice the preservative, the perishable.
The dichotomous crystal.

In the lonesome archives, yellowing photographs of men
with shark-toothed saws
harvesting the lake at Bell Ewart and Beaverton.
Employees of the Lake Simcoe
Ice Company, the Spring Water
Ice Corporation, the vast Ice Union.
The blocks shipped as far as Cleveland.
Box cars packed tight,
cubes covered in sawdust, gold filaments.
Ghost breath of the anonymous
who loaded and groaned.

26

In August that frozen harvest
felt like the unexpected breeze
from a mountain top. That's how it is
in this climate of opposites: when the sun
bears down and everyone is out speaking
you need to be reminded of the reticence of January,
the cold, inescapable truth of February
so you can picture all the green as white,
so you can see being as non-being.

27

Where were any of us in August 1615
when Étienne Brûlé led Samuel de Champlain
to the narrows between Simcoe and Couchiching?
Network of giant stakes,
the watchful weirs and wide wattles,
and the muscle-bulging fish nets
flashing their hologram of scales.

Brûlé the convert, naked
from the waist down, feathers
dangling from his matted hair.
A century before Rousseau
he wears the rings of the noble savage,
explains the Huron fear that the great harvest
might end, and warns of wastage,
warns of offending the God
of the Nets.

28

How could he see
the small tributaries of the Black River
stoked with ammonia, phosphates, PCBs?
Our luminous cocktail. How could he know
those river deities would one day be requisitioned by
the Sunlight Detergent Company, the Simcoe
Dairy Factory, the Georgina Township
Water Authority? The brackish surface
a deep bottle green breeding algae on the bleached banks,
cotton-like strands melting to slime
between trembling fingers.
Our horror ditch.

29

No prophet, he recorded Huron maidens
paddling through August's early morning mist
willing to offer themselves to the Spirit of the Nets.

And so too I once drifted,
watching a girl chew on a stalk of grass.
Behind her, a tire swing,
a sagging shack, her father's rusted
Mercury on concrete blocks.
Her perfect pale legs.

Pangs of Eros
rising out of the mulch,
fetor of bilge and rotted fish —
erect petals of the water lilies.

30

Lie back, Canadian Cavalcanti
and pluck river sounds from the strings of your Yamaha
for Rebecca. Or Diana.

Perhaps in the cicada chorus,
in the bullfrog's signature key,
she will return

Her peeling sunburnt shoulder,
tanned calves.

First love. Last.

But no river flows backwards.
No river resuscitates its dead.

31

Meditate instead upon the Cartesian boulder
half darkened by water
half blanched faceless by the
simmering sun. Whatever changes rock incurs
are not obvious to the naked eye,
not apprehended in a single human life.
You'd need the vision of Ha-Shem to record
that tenor of erosion, that symphony
of silent reduction played out in freeze-up and thaw.

As for the boulder
stuck fast within its nature —
ask that prisoner and anchor
how many of the drowning
reach with their last grasp
for its hardness.

32

Here memory is short-lived.
Shallow land, rock too close to surface.
And our river — an amnesiac:
her biography, mere movement.

We're left with a bumpkin nation,
fanatics of the Brewery,
devotees of Hockey
jet-skiers and snow-mobilers.
Award-winning poets who can't rhyme a line of verse.
And worse.

Only one political visionary over the past
half century. PET — the tough shrug,
the open human. The rest —
hucksters, pollsters, launderers,
bag men undoing the nation.

Carry them, Black River,
as detritus
        to Detroit.

33

It is 1838 and St. George's Anglican Church
is finally complete.
In the township, the crickets
tap their warnings.
                        The cemetery is ready
for its guests.
                  What a sorry mix:
these committed bones and the towering
non-denominational pines.
And that scrap of a Union Jack
fluttering inside each chest
as boxed redcoats are let down
into the black earth of Khartoum, Madras.
And later,
those bloody harbingers — fragments
of Flanders.

34

And look, there are the newcomers
huddled on a Halifax pier,
each clutching a passport of despair.
They can see all the way into the country,
all the way to Black River.
Years later I stand with them on winter ice
huddled in a heated makeshift
warmed by Seagram & Sons
brooding over lines sunk in dark punctures,
imagining those aquatic angels hovering in the frigid depths
like God's good intentions
just out of reach

sending me to the Committee of Spiritual
Adjustments, the Association for Disinherited
Wisdom, the Silent Heritage Foundation,
the Township
of Lost Fellowship.

35

By the river bank, branches
of the massive willows
thrummed by wind.
Their high hollow whistling,
harrowing the late afternoons.

Is that what the psalmist meant
by his 'harps upon the willow'?

Those captives
weeping by the rivers of Babylon
were 'required to sing a song'.
Required by whom?
By 'those that wasted us'.

How to sing the Lord's song in a strange land?
Is that not the all-time question?
Do not look for answers in the
promiscuous river
possessed but not possessing.

36

What river ran through the village of Lipsk
near Grodno
where my great-grandparents
gathered ghosts over candles?
Wind through the Polish flax fields
a sea
      yellow as David's Star

crossed in no time by dark chariots
filled with Pharaoh's executioners.

They left my progenitors gasping
in rivulets of blood.

Little men, revving the engines
of their spiked chariots
                  deaf
to the long condemnation
of the diasporic wind.

37

My grandfather's nose and bronzed skin
akin to the Indian's: the Sioux-Jew,
the Huron-Hebrew. All those years as a tailor
had not rendered him stranger to water.
Each time he approached it his eyes quickened —
a Baltic blue. Mr Nimble Thimble,
he'd thread a hook, first try.
His cast, effortless, making you think
all those years by the rattling sewing machine
had been seriously misspent.
Pious piscator, he was no talker.
He'd stare deadpan at the horizon,
the fleshy button of his thumb
pressed against the pulse of the line,
his ear tuned to the reel's ratchet.
All present tense.

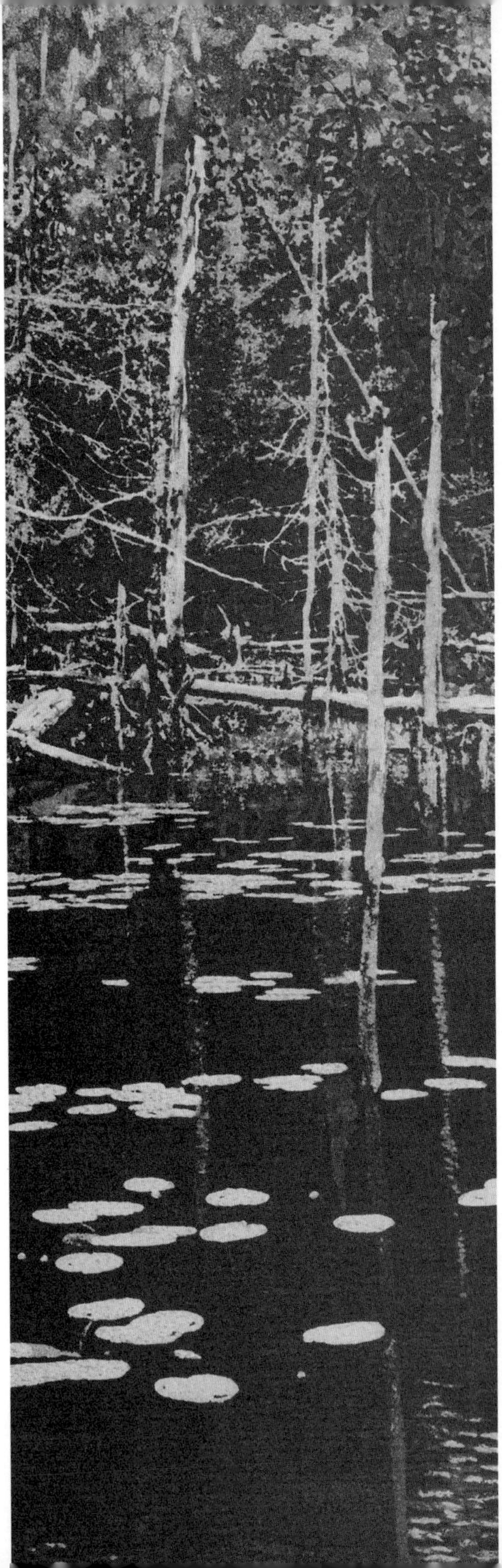

38

And down below, the baby bass,
nosing, touching tentative,
their fan-like tails fringed with Japanese ink —
silk in the shallow pools.

Shadows of the hanging willow
cast over them,
shade them in the aquatic cradle
as they sway to no music,
startle and split,
then regroup
each staring into its mirror image.

What do they ponder,
suspended there like little harbingers?

Were they too
fostered by beauty and fear?

When they grow
they travel alone
in the school of their solitude,
grim-mouthed, gills kneading their being,
foraging through the frigid gloom.

39

Piscator — the spirit of God
first moved upon the water
and the *mysterium* of fish:
their long glassy stares into the rippling
mirror. When did I first fall in love with *The Compleat Angler*,
Walton's worm diary, his snap-wrist homage to poetry?
Imagine life as a chub, as a bolting minnow,
or as a chirruping gracehoper, alluring one inch
above water. This angling —
like some English Tao: how to spend life on a river bank
without falling in (felicitous compromise
between contemplation and action).

40

(What we have here is a rough approximation
of the numinous, as in the paintings of Shalom
of Safed, or in 'The Miraculous Draught of Fishes'
by Conrad Witz. But how to be God-centred
with Google, as if deadpan glass and hard-drive hum
could be any long-term consolation?
Lovely the way it flows onto the screen
though you are unlikely to download
Eden or Zion from this Net so easily accessed
and deluged with everyday demons.)

41

At sunset, the river was smeared red:
Blake's Adona — the dipped foot
of the bleeding god. Adonis, Adona, Adonai —
link between Greek and Jew.
So, Phaedrus, how's by you?

42

I was a stranger in a new world, mercantile,
paternal, caught between the umbilical of the
biblical and the cadence of decadence —
a Now Dance at the altar, perhaps.

43

And whose river is it anyway?
Ultimately, it belongs to the lonely,
to those heavier than air,
                        lighter than water.

Its seasons are a translation, or a shifting
from one language to another, or the movement
from shouts to speech,
                        from speech
to whispers,
           whispers to gestures —
pantomime of winter:

wind shaking the glazed aspen,
the whitened sumac.

44

For whose soul isn't described
in Hunter's Simcoe Survey of 1893?
Strata of silt, clay, limestone, shale —
the hardening rivers below the river.

Stop and search beneath life's flux
if you wish to discover your will,
your forbearance.

Then there's the truck I spotted
on the Baseline Road
barrelling along with its strata
of flattened wrecks:
each layer, a crushed metal memory capsule —
the confessions, the tunes, the laughter,
the pleas, the back seat
lovemaking.
All of it carried off down the river of rural roads.

45

And if nothing stands still —
Nihil. Nihil.

While Provincial dignitaries
and their families were picnicking on
Strawberry Island in the summer of 1885
(ties, vests, bustles, corsets)

Friedrich Nietzsche
was bringing down Europe
with his pen.

We are strained through his moustache.
We sit in his twilight on lawn chairs
speaking like shades
until the mosquitoes come.

O bless them. They are like a New World refutation
with their consistent hum.

Perfect as a plague.

Our bloody rivulets
pierced by the needle-nosed
messengers of sense.

46

Some might wish to stand in a castle
and gaze down upon the tumultuous sea.
A castle, immense,
obsessed with its own idea of firmness.

And a wind, blowing in an angel
who urges us to take down holy dictation.

What I have is a shed by a slow-moving river:
phlox, skunkweed, tiger lilies, wild grass.

To hear an angel — now that would be a trip —
instead of this slow gurgling,
these indecipherable bird cries,
the soporific rush of weekend traffic.

Perhaps this land is too green for him.
Perhaps he requires
a sun-blasted Sinai, some vast
urban desolation,
                        hollowed cathedrals and
castles, the long-standing spectre
of disillusionment.

47

This maple leaf a warning —
no world culture here, old friend.
Acknowledge the banality of regions
and townships, your lordships
and Queen Bees.
Stop playing it so safe. Stop
birding your time with flaky
inconsequential lyrical trills.
Scrabblers and literary mufti,
Harbourfront's a front. That whale-man —
a commissar of the bland literati.
Two — count 'em — 'must read' novels.
Per week.

48

Be like Mr Turtle,
His shell is swamp green.
His fetid underside, corn yellow
sunburst orange,
a matrix of dark lines —
fate's partitions.

Old as Tyrannous Rex,
(whom he outlived).
Slower than Achilles
and while less famous,
more durable.

A disciple of Zeno,
he knows that the distance between
the slowest and the fastest does not vanish

hence he has no need to bargain with any god
or goddess.

        His codger's neck
and bald droplet head,
his black blinking eyes —
a testament.

Over the world
he drags his weight, his shelter,

leaving his signature
in the dust.

49

Or forget Zeno's paradox and say motion exists.
Ask anyone who's had shin splints, torn tendons.
I set out before dawn along the river's edge
At first I am stiff and question my purpose.
Soon I settle into a rhythm
that has the power to take me anywhere:
flexed calves, syncopated breath,
zone of pure being.
I recall Whitman's marathon man: 'lightly
closed fists and arms partially
raised'. There you have it,
the master's sufficient phrase.
Have I really been sold better soles?
I see myself running through the centuries,
purified by movement. Am I fleeing
or aspiring, am I departing or arriving.
Or am I somewhere in between?

50

What I contend with is something quite unlike
your typical Orphic invocation
where an unshaven dickmaster
wah-wahs his sunburst Stratocaster
to the undulating, adulating herd.

I contend with that pernicious voice
(whose is it?) whispering 'Nothing lasts.'
Yet notes persist, as recorded in *The Universal Enquirer*,
(Severed Head Sings Down River!) —
our press that never goes out of business.

51

Any river becomes black
when it drowns a poet.
Yet, how things change ...

Qu Yuan, in double exile,
drowned himself in the Milui river
near Xiangshui. Peasants
dropped rice dumplings
wrapped in reed leaves so that fish
would not nibble at his corpse.

And Li Po's disciples wept a river
after the master leaned too far
to catch moon's reflection ...

Celan. Berryman.
Lost to the isolating currents.

The American's final wave
to an imaginary friend.

Celan's terse swan dive
into the war-haunted Seine,

his anonymous corpse, unclaimed

floating
past the cold blue berets.

52

'O Sleepless as the river,' cried Hart Crane
In the end he gave himself to water.
We build bridges to one another,
to the gay tormented ghosts
who are tireless as the current
that threatens and sustains

Klein's blue and bloated suicides

or Woolf collecting crow flowers,
'dead man's fingers',
her smock spread wide and mermaid-like
heavy with drink, pulled down to muddy death.

And here, over Scottish settlers' bones,
vascular, turbid, Black River
lifting from its rocky bed
these spectral hymns.

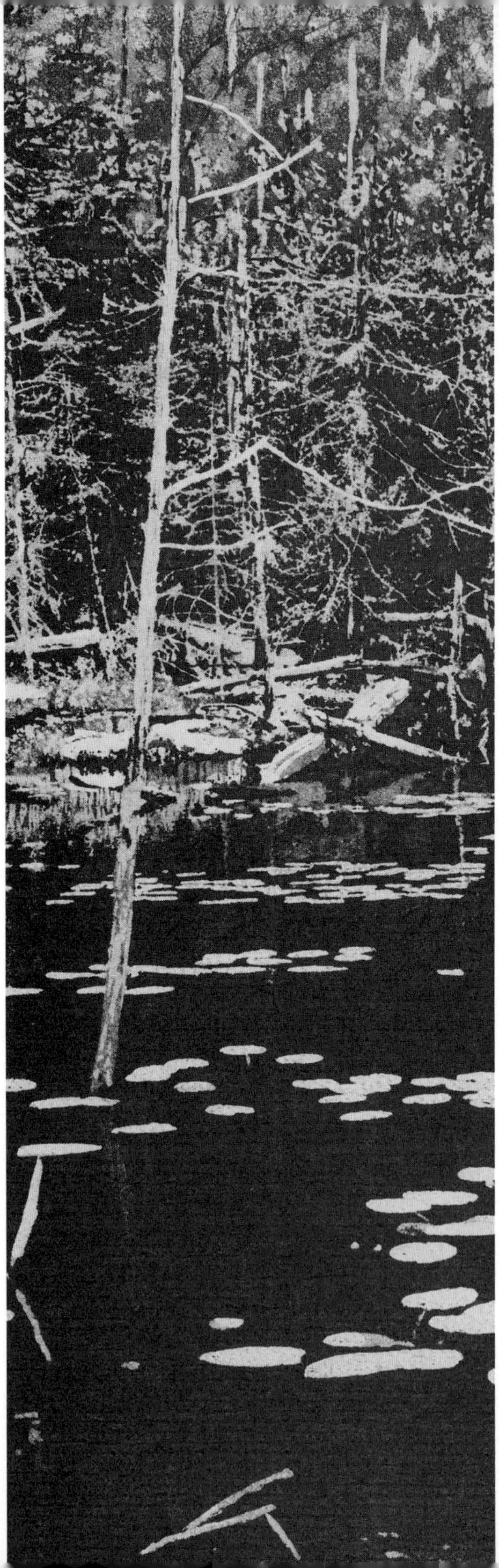

53

Native masks, cleaved
from the brooding tree:
the Shrieker, the Shocked,
or famous False Face,
nose and mouth hideously askew,
the one who ran up against the impossible —

Masks, given to those who went under
who dreamt themselves backwards

healers
      who heal themselves
by healing others

the wood's grain, brilliant,
burnished with the voice
of the wounded.

Is it dry grass, is it the hair
of enemies or loved ones
that flows from the head
down these hardened cheeks?

54

Coming up
from the Commercial Valley Road
into the Lucky Seven Mall. Sutton,
Keswick, Newmarket, Aurora — the lights
burn 24/7. *Come unto me ye who labour
and are heavy burdened.* But not through
the Dark Net, vast, anarchic, pornography
of Gallup. Democracy
our abuse of statistics. Shore
to shore, river unto river, and
peer to peer.
Menschen Fressers.
Our cannibal galaxy.

55

Online: Not the trout.
Not the brooding bass. Not the sunburst
perch at the end of your hair's-breadth filament
but an electric light show, *amigo*,
promising connection, not
redemption. My barque, my moving
masque, casting a shadow over the
sinking river floor, dark
in a different way: murky and
inviolable.

56

It is October. Autumn's rot.
After a dry summer, so few colours.
Everything on the verge.

                    Your darkness
hasn't altered. Maybe that is why I think of you
as Lethe, swallowing little cousins and those
wriggling sunfish we returned to you as a gift.
Not even pollution
                halts your momentum.

Perhaps with Zen I could learn
to quit figuring you, see you as River,
delight in being

forget those photographs of neighbours
holding the stringer, arms straining with
grim-mouthed bass.

'By the waters of Lethe I saw the future.'
Thank you, Pan Milosz. That is a fine Polish
twist. And what shall we,
who spring from this continent,
say of true forgetfulness?

57

As one grows older
does the water clear?

58

And what then is memory to one man?
Time flowing along his inner river —
a world to be mused over,
winding the same curves again
and again.
            The characters on shore, may,
with age, be seen in a new light,
not as one's projections, less determinate —
universal players
                behind the Great Curtain.

In that small habitation, too much
mime: the Enraged, the Stooped, the Sour,
the Avenger. Oh, let it go.
But it is *my* wound, Sir,
my cricket sound.

59

The whirligigs' determined confusion
and the flash of the leopard frog
before it vanishes, not forever,
but a means to endure.

The wind is like a mother
searching for her stolen children.
I can hear her low wail
through the flexile leaves.
And the river current, desperate,
rushing over rough stones.

Then why do summers seem to pass
with a sumptuous gentleness?

At dusk I sit on the screened porch
and listen to the river. I hear
a solitary splash
while down in the black bindweed
a multitude of lives writhe and resist.

60

I know that this river is not the Jordan
and that Sutton is not Jerusalem.

And I know that the small water-strider
pulsing its way through the murky Ecclesia
is not the Angel of Redemption.

The sagging wharves and driftwood
are pale as spirits that will not fade,
that get harder as they get older.

And still I enter the canoe
that is ribbed like Adam,
its gunwales weathered, its thwarts
webbed.
I stir the water with my will
and peer down into the Final Registry.

Lamentations of bullfrogs.
The cry of a chain saw.
The odious mixture of cars and nature
on the back roads, winding through
the Unlimited Diaspora.

The red eye of the sun
watches me
between trees

and I ask the Master of the Net,
my *Malus Angelus*,
What is the purpose of this language?

A harsh contrivance
of spirit against Death

The flawed and the unfinished,
emanations
from the throats of the broken

fanning out
like a wake toward shore.

ACKNOWLEDGEMENTS

The author wishes to thank the Canada Council and the Ontario Arts Council for their assistance during the writing of this book. Section 35 first appeared in *Parchment*; section 48 first appeared in *The Antigonish Review*.

The cover, and interior images, are taken from an etching and aquatint entitled *Where Sound Is Crystalline* (15.5" x 23.5") by George Raab, a Canadian printmaker whose original wilderness landscape etchings have earned him an international reputation. Raab's studio and home is located on a small farm in the picturesque village of Millbrook, Ontario, northeast of Toronto.

ADAM SHERMAN

ABOUT THE AUTHOR

Kenneth Sherman was born in Toronto in 1950. He has a BA from York University, where he studied with Eli Mandel and Irving Layton, and an MA in English Literature from the University of Toronto. While a student at York, Sherman co-founded and edited the literary journal *Waves*.

From 1974 to 1975 he travelled extensively through Asia. He is a full-time faculty member at Sheridan College where he teaches Communications; he also teaches a course in creative writing at the University of Toronto.

In 1982, Sherman was writer-in-residence at Trent University. In 1986 he was invited by the Chinese government to lecture on contemporary Canadian literature at universities and government institutions in Beijing. In 1988, he received a Canada Council grant to travel through Poland and Russia. This experience inspired several of the essays in his book *Void and Voice* (1998).

Sherman, author of the acclaimed *Words for Elephant Man*, and *The Well: New and Selected Poems*, lives in Toronto with his wife, Marie, an artist.